This library edition published in 2014 by Walter Foster Publishing,
a division of Quarto Publishing Group USA Inc.
3 Wrigley, Suite A
Irvine, CA 92618

Nickelodeon
nick.com

Distributed in the United States and Canada by
Lerner Publisher Services
241 First Avenue North
Minneapolis, MN 55401 U.S.A.
www.lernerbooks.com

First Library Edition

Library of Congress Cataloging-in-Publication Data

How to draw Nickelodeon Teenage Mutant Ninja Turtles : / step-by-step
illustrations by Nino Navarra. -- First library edition.
    pages cm
 Includes bibliographical references and index.
ISBN 978-1-93958-117-4
1. Teenage Mutant Ninja Turtles (Fictitious characters)--Juvenile
literature. 2. Cartooning--Technique--Juvenile literature. 3. Teenage
Mutant Ninja Turtles (Television program : 2012-)--Juvenile literature.
I. Navarra, Nino, illustrator.
 NC1764.8.T44H69 2013
 741.5'1--dc23
                                                                    2013011666

102014
19040

9 8 7 6 5 4 3

HOW TO DRAW

nickelodeon™
TEENAGE MUTANT NINJA
TURTLES

STEP-BY-STEP
ILLUSTRATIONS BY
NIÑO NAVARRA

TABLE OF CONTENTS

Rising from the sewers, four fun-loving and hard-fighting brothers—Leonardo, Donatello, Michelangelo, and Raphael—strive to master martial arts while protecting their family, friends, city, and the world from ever-increasing threats. They are

TEENAGE MUTANT NINJA TURTLES™

It all started when a ninjutsu master named Hamato Yoshi bought four regular-sized turtles from a pet store in Chinatown. He wanted pets, but he got more than that when two human-looking creatures doused Yoshi and his turtles with strange Ooze. A mutagenic Ooze. A liquid from beyond that transformed the DNA of any living thing that it touched.

Having just come into contact with an alley rat, Yoshi grew a tail, a covering of thick fur, and long teeth. Yoshi was no longer Yoshi. He was now a mutated human/rat hybrid known as Splinter.

And his pet turtles were no longer average turtles. They grew to more than five feet tall, and they developed a human skeletal form and increased intelligence. They were mutants. With their shells and newfound muscles, they were stronger and tougher than almost any other animal on the planet.

Splinter retreated to his den in the sewers and raised the turtles as his own children. There, he taught the brothers the discipline, philosophy, and martial arts they would need to survive and thrive.

SIZE CHART

When drawing, it's important to understand a character's proportions (the correct size of things compared with other things). Use this height chart to help you draw the characters' proportions correctly.

LEO

DONNIE

MIKEY

RAPH

APRIL

SPLINTER

KRAANG

SHREDDER

TOOLS + MATERIALS

You'll need to gather a few simple drawing tools before you begin. Start with a regular pencil and eraser so you can easily erase any mistakes. Make sure you have a sharpener and ruler too. To add color to your drawings, grab some markers, colored pencils, crayons, or even acrylic or watercolor paint.

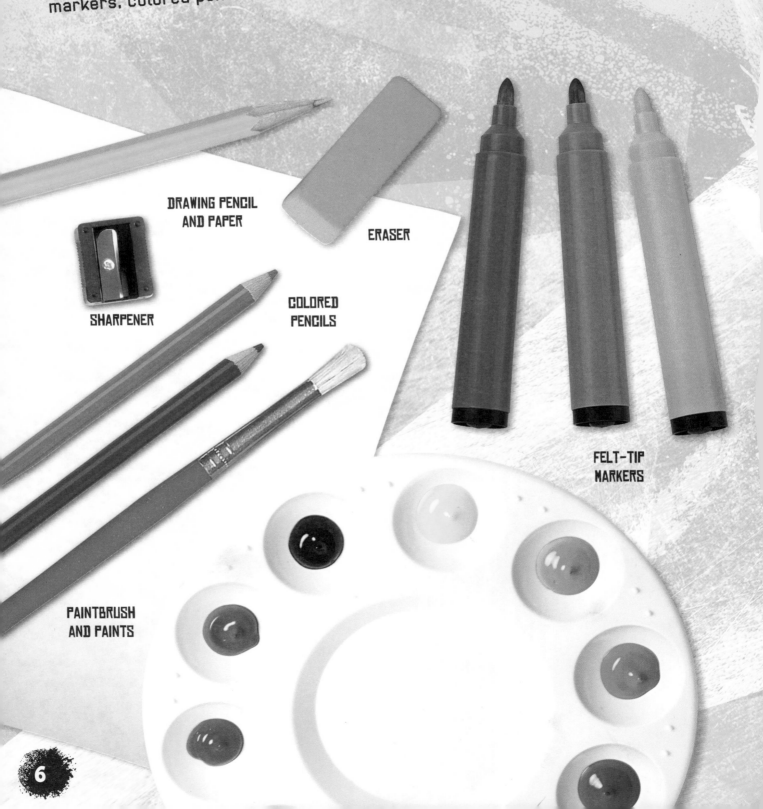

DRAWING PENCIL
AND PAPER

ERASER

SHARPENER

COLORED
PENCILS

FELT-TIP
MARKERS

PAINTBRUSH
AND PAINTS

HOW TO USE THIS BOOK

You can draw any of the characters in this book by following these simple steps.

STEP 1

Start your drawing in the middle of the paper so you won't run out of room.

STEP 2

Each new step appears in blue, so you'll always know what to draw next.

STEP 3

Take your time and copy the blue lines.

STEP 4

Refine the lines of your drawing. Then add the details.

STEP 5

Darken the lines you want to keep and erase the rest.

STEP 6

Add color to your drawing with colored pencils, markers, paints, or crayons!

LEONARDO

Leo is a stand-up guy and master of the katana, the most legendary and noble of Japanese weapons. A born leader, Leonardo is learning from Splinter how to guide and inspire his brothers. And it works. Usually. Well, sometimes.

Legs and arms are tubes that flare
out at the base

4

3

9

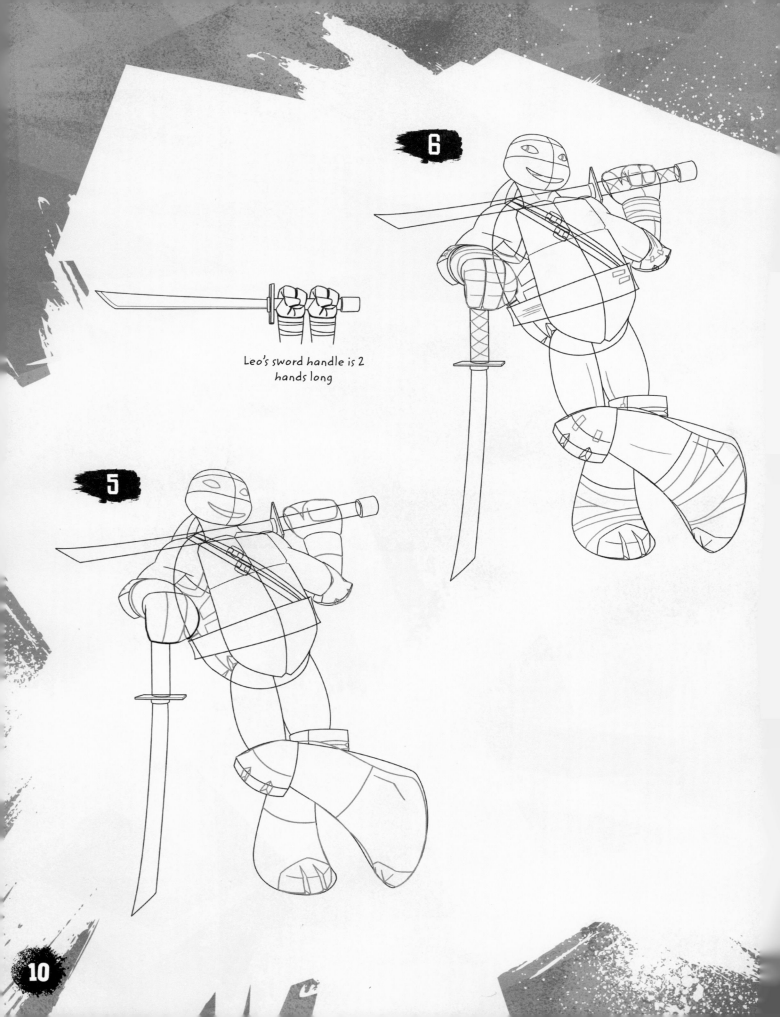

6

5

Leo's sword handle is 2 hands long

Leo's basic shapes are squares and rectangles

7

LEONARDO
IN ACTION

Traditionally, the Japanese believed that a sword, like Leo's katana, had a soul. When matched with a great warrior, it was an almost spiritual token of power. Wielding a katana is a great responsibility.

1

2

3

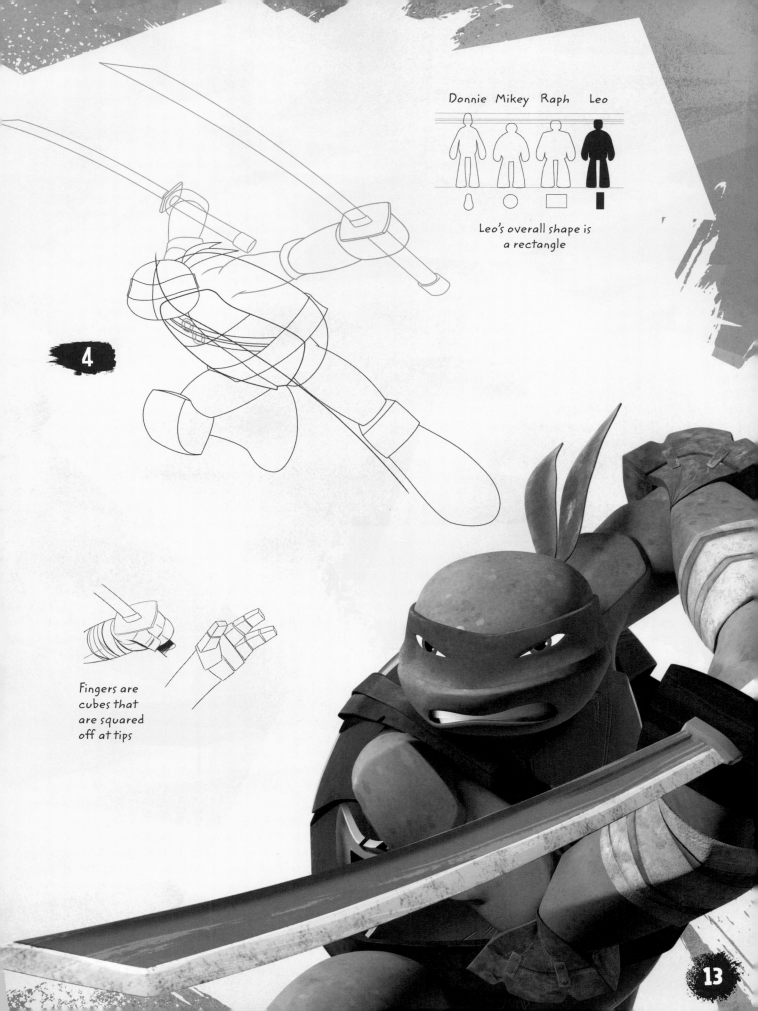

Donnie	Mikey	Raph	Leo

Leo's overall shape is a rectangle

4

Fingers are cubes that are squared off at tips

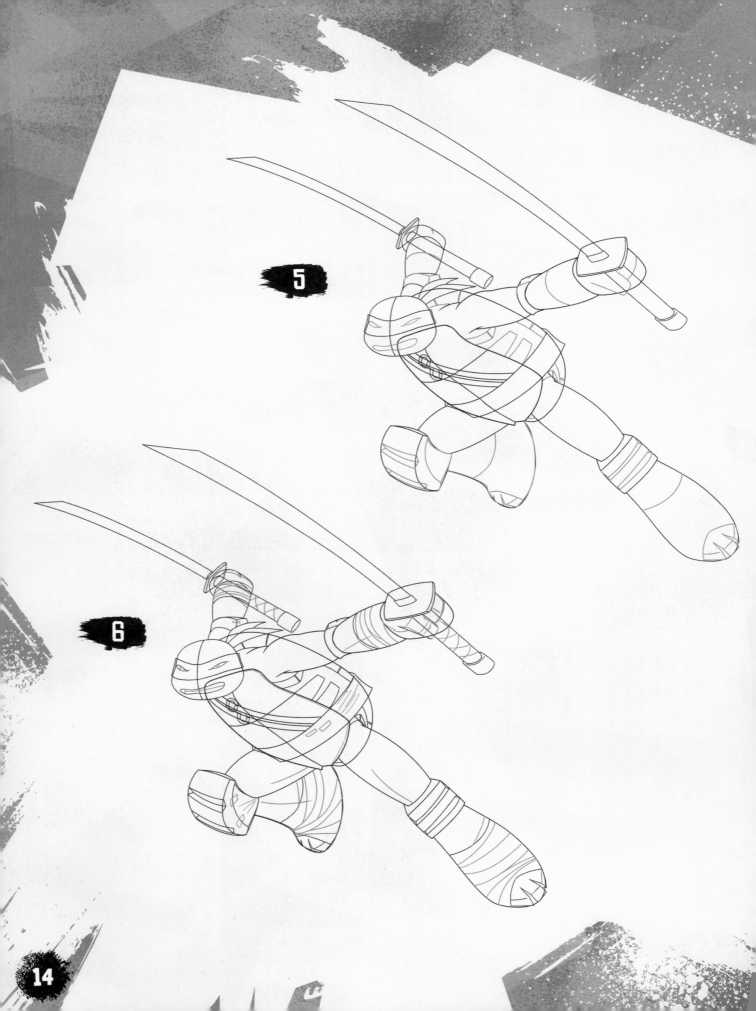

5

6

7

RAPHAEL

The hotheaded warrior of the group, Raph knows his skills with the sai are unmatched by anyone. So why can't his brothers acknowledge that and recognize him as the best? The only way to make them understand is to be the greatest.

1

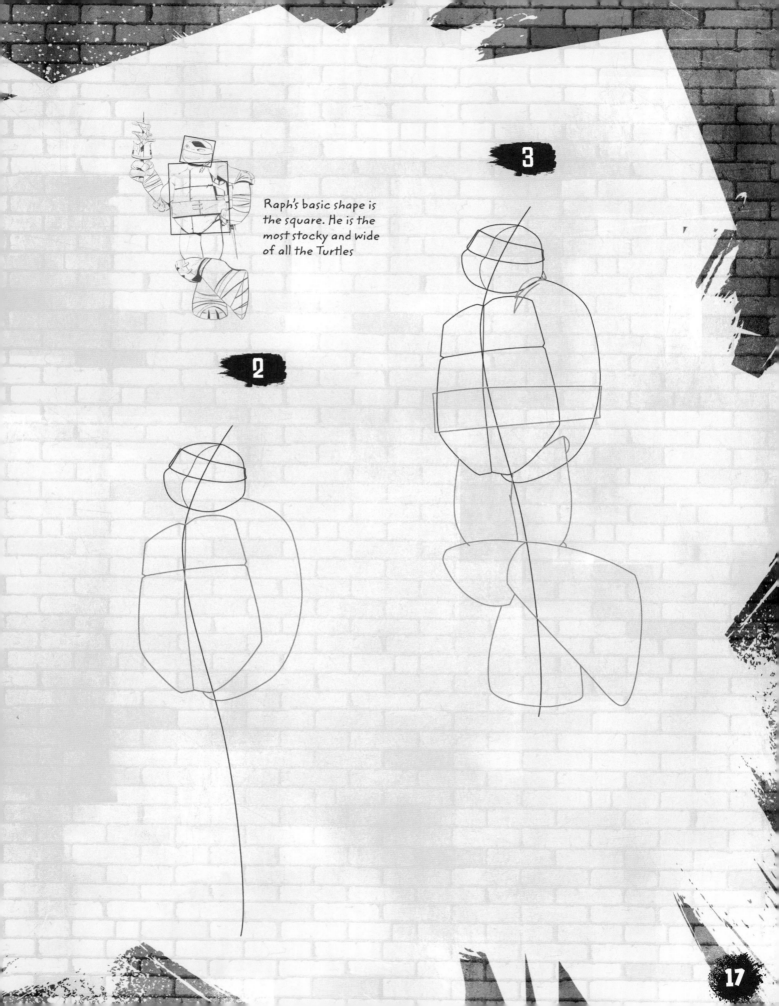

Raph's basic shape is the square. He is the most stocky and wide of all the Turtles

2

3

4

Raph has lots of
battle damage on his
shell and clothing

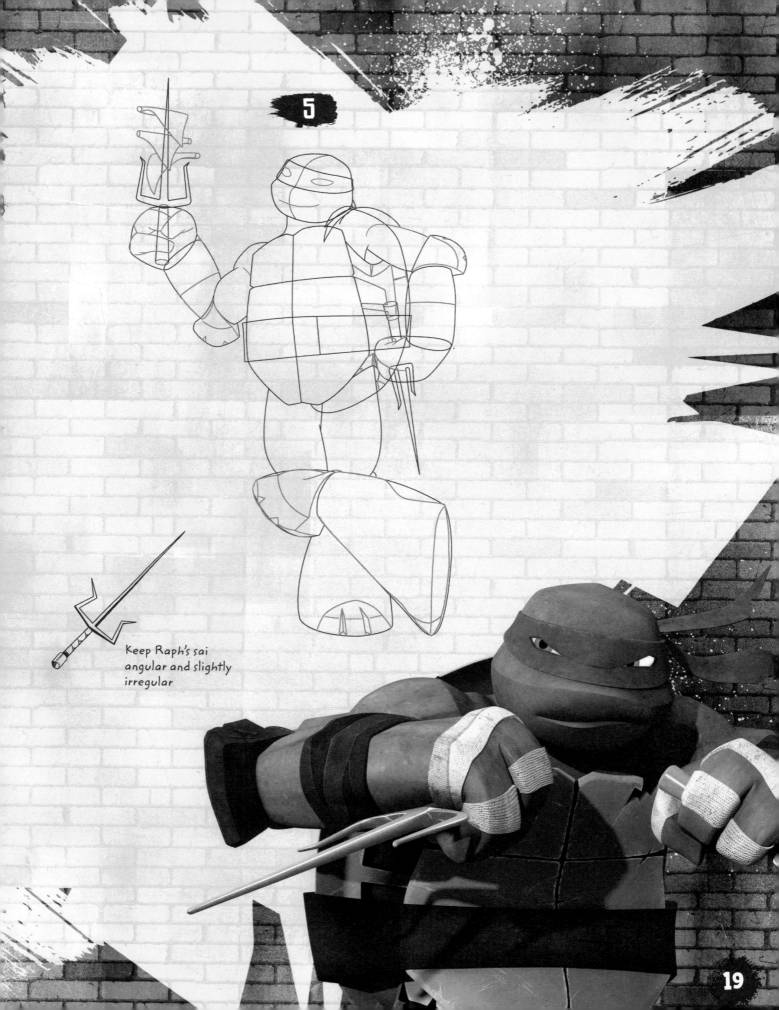

5

Keep Raph's sai angular and slightly irregular

RAPHAEL

Raphael's sai allows him to attack, trap, and block his opponents. Sais are great for striking; they're unmatched in close combat—and excellent as forks for eating pizza.

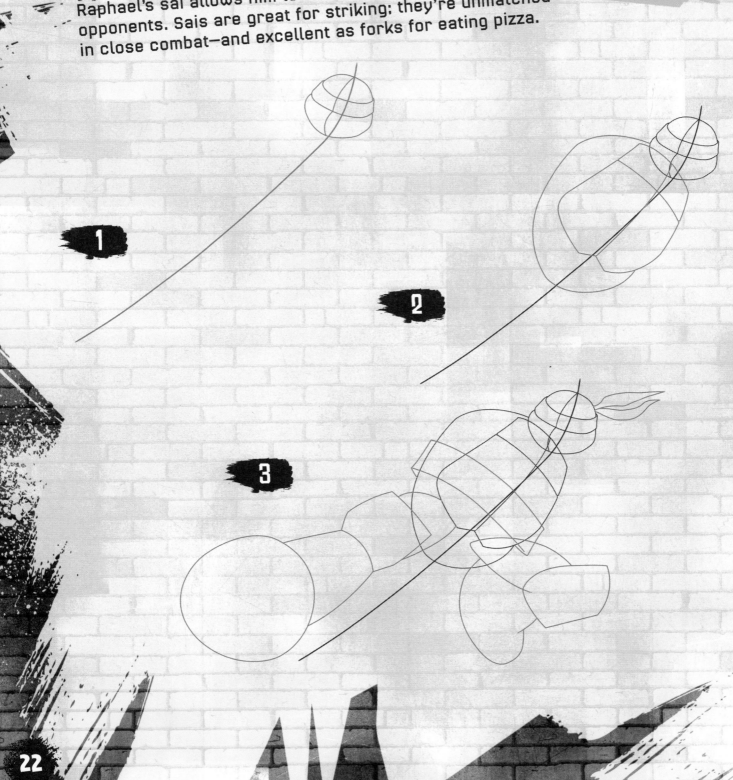

1

2

3

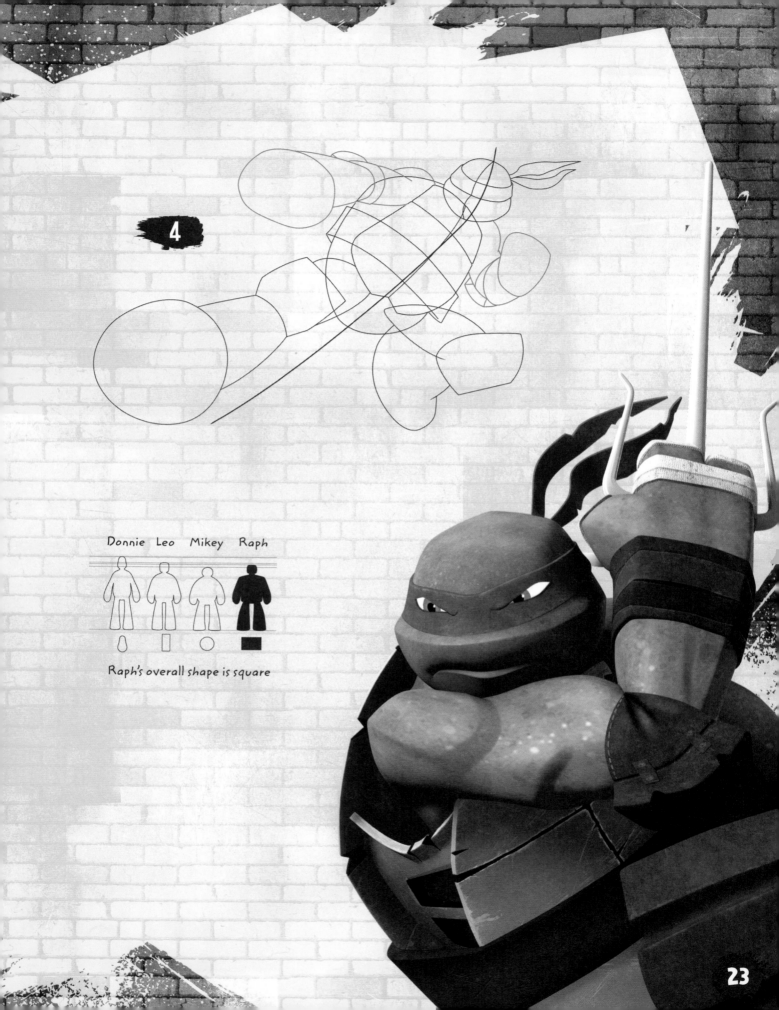

4

Donnie   Leo   Mikey   Raph

Raph's overall shape is square

23

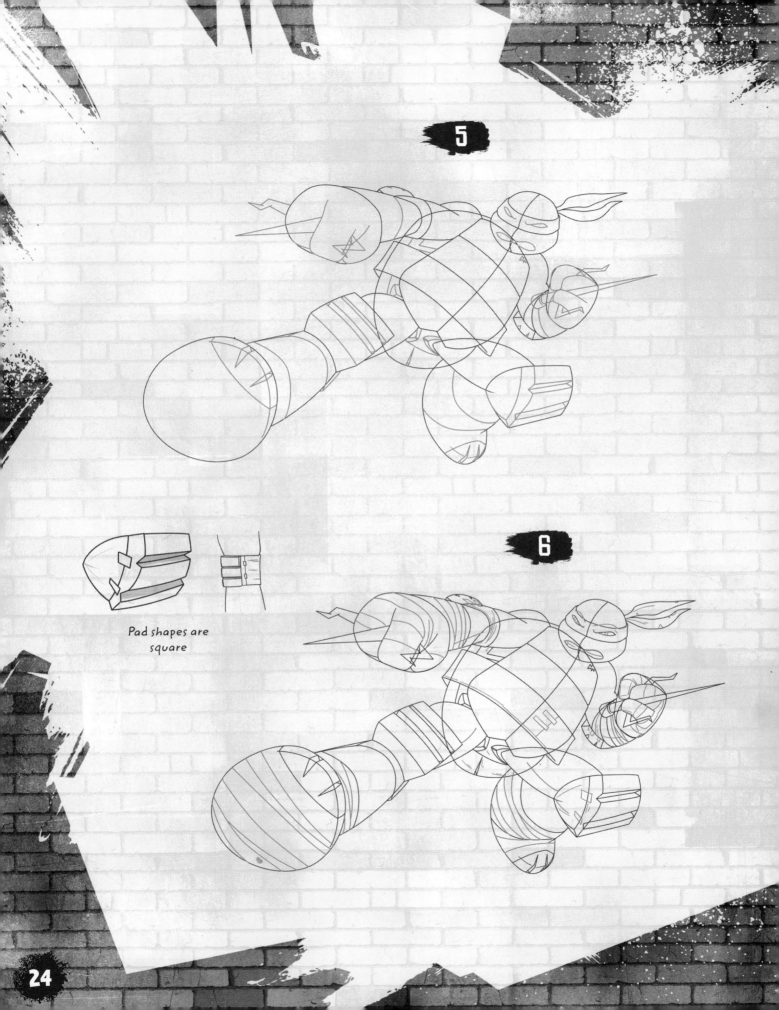

5

6

Pad shapes are
square

7

MICHELANGELO

Party animal, practical joker, nunchuks master: all of these words apply to Mikey. He is a master ninja, so why don't his brothers listen to his awesome ideas? He makes up for it by trying to get them to laugh, either with him or (mostly) at him.

1

2

Keep weapon
shapes simple

4

3

5

6

Mikey is the roundest
of the Turtles

7

MICHELANGELO

Though Mikey is the goofball of the group, his nunchuks are a difficult weapon to master. Nunchuks are exceptional for striking, but they are also perfect for distracting one's enemy.

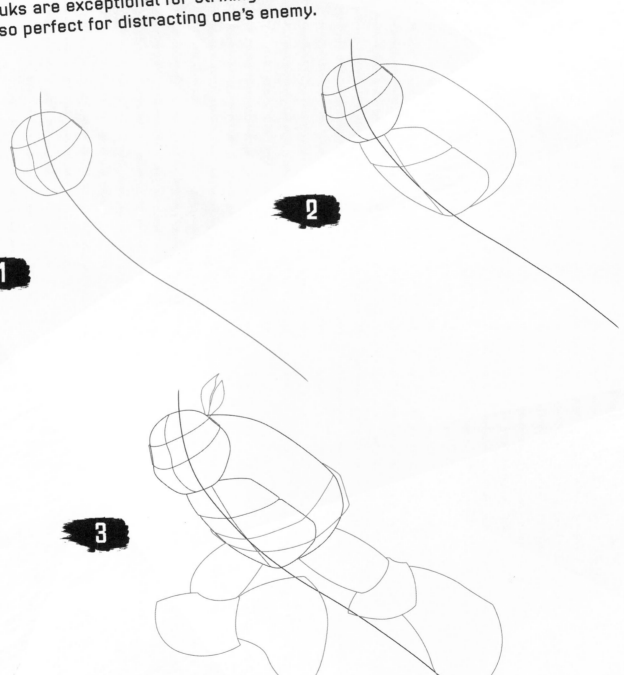

1

2

3

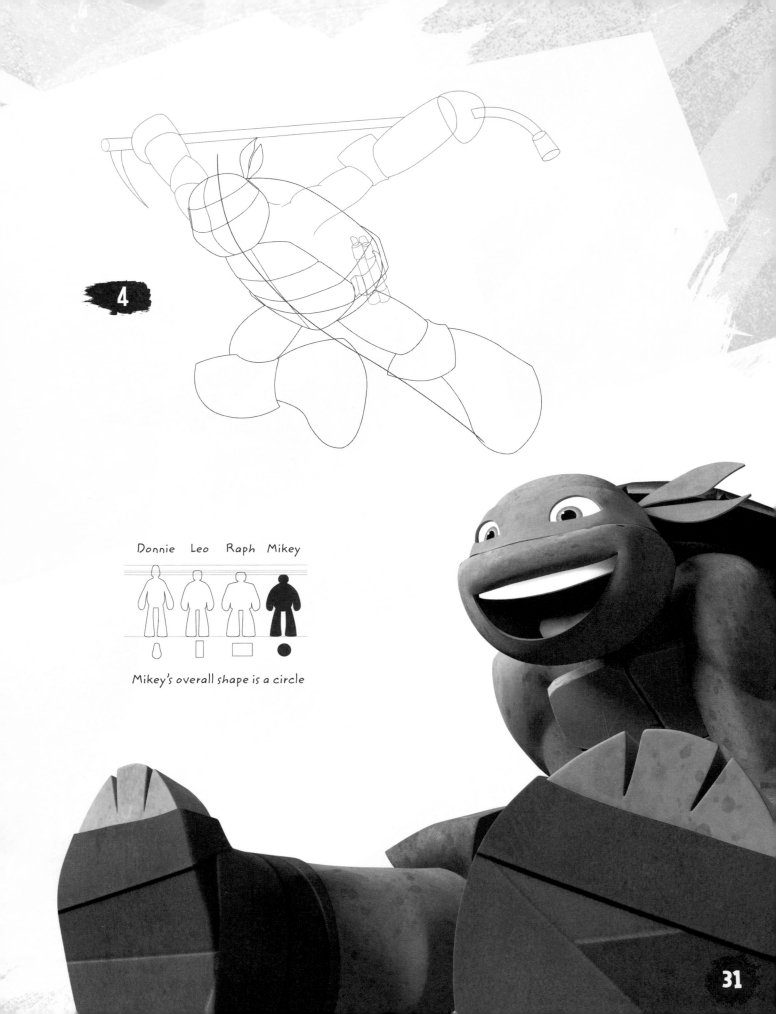

4

Donnie Leo Raph Mikey

Mikey's overall shape is a circle

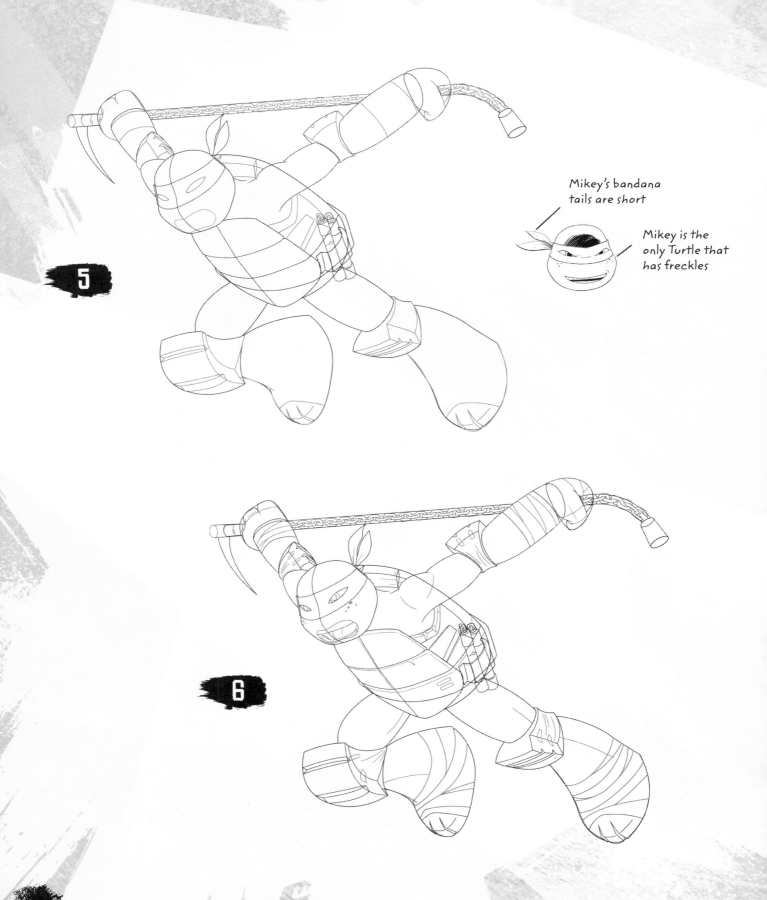

5

Mikey's bandana tails are short

Mikey is the only Turtle that has freckles

6

7

DONATELLO

Donnie is the brains of this outfit. He's as good a fighter as his brothers, but his real strength is his mind. His "do-it-yourself" attitude leads to exploration of the sewers, reconstructing garbage into computers, and making a TV with three whole channels. The only thing he can't figure out is how to get the Turtles' human friend, April, to notice him.

1

2

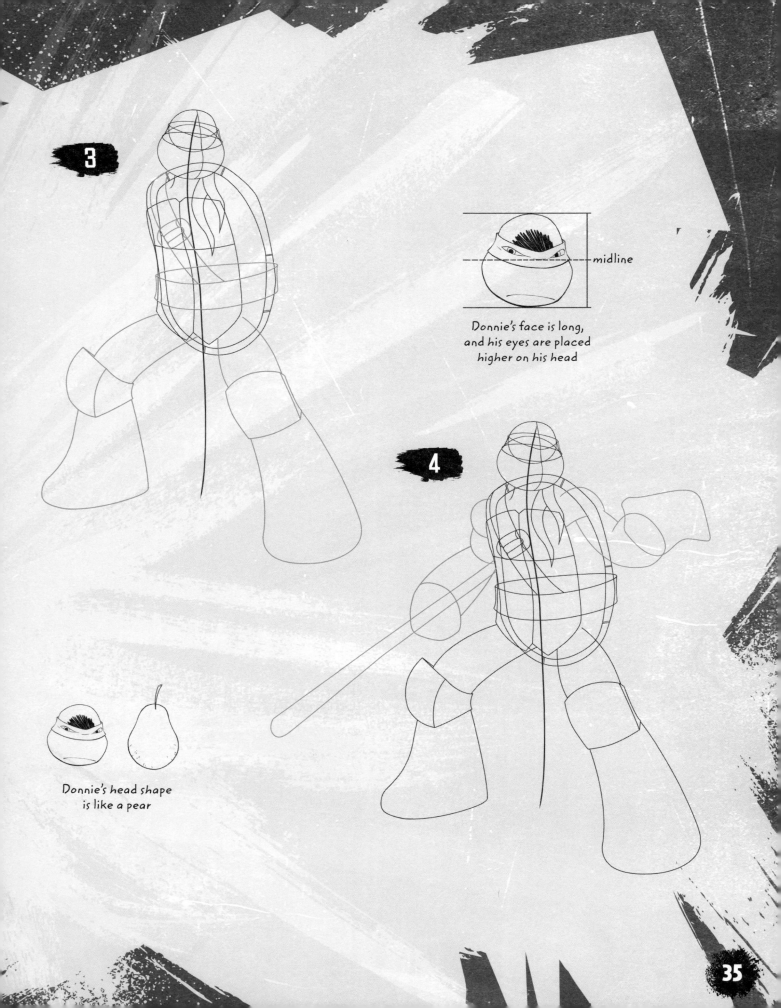

3

midline

Donnie's face is long,
and his eyes are placed
higher on his head

4

Donnie's head shape
is like a pear

5

6

DONATELLO
IN ACTION

Donnie's bo-staff allows him to keep his opponents at a distance while he determines how best to take advantage of the weapon's unmatched versatility: attacking, defending, or even vaulting over an enemy to escape.

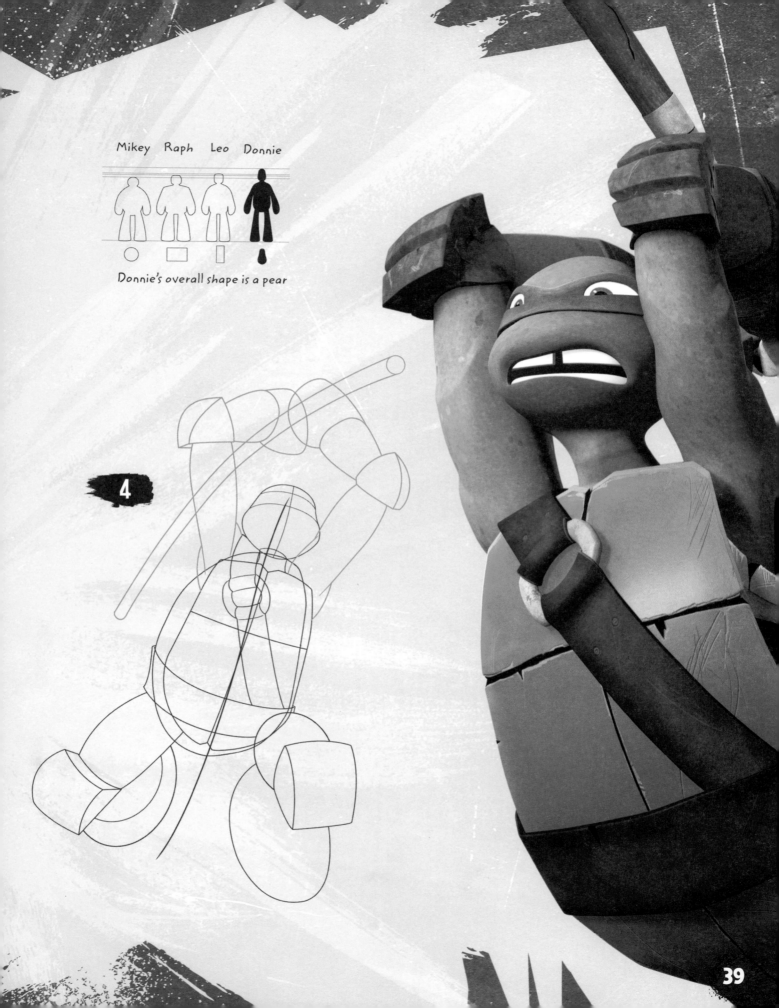

Mikey Raph Leo Donnie

Donnie's overall shape is a pear

4

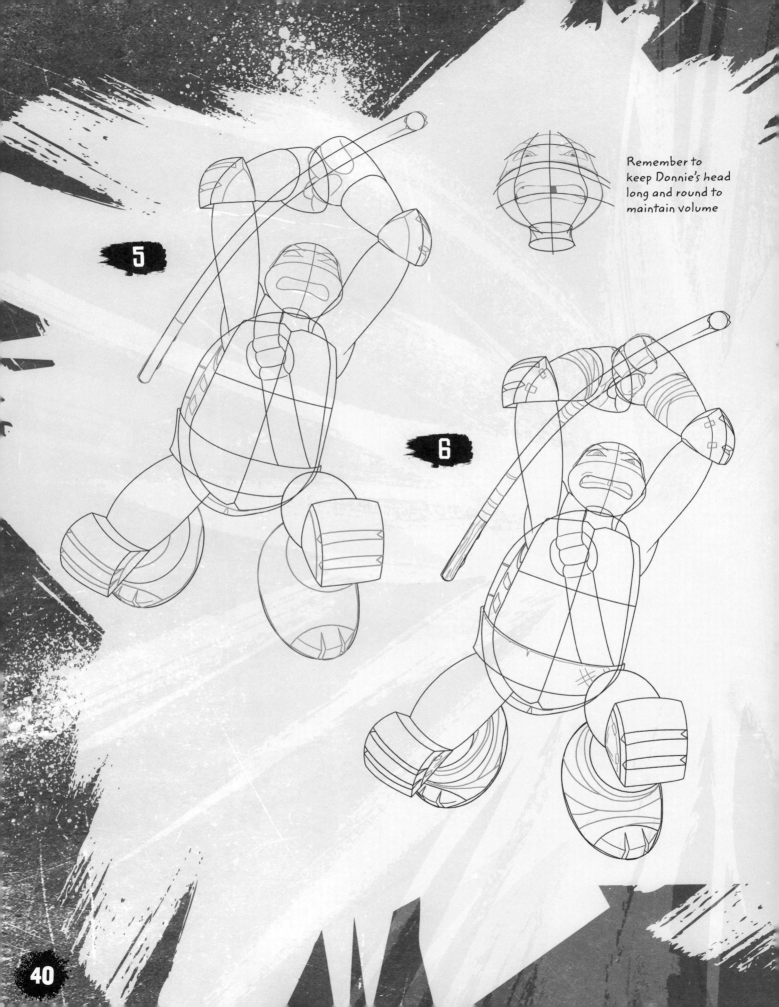

5

6

Remember to
keep Donnie's head
long and round to
maintain volume

7

SPLINTER

The mutated human/rat known as Splinter is devoted to teaching the Turtles the skills they need in order to survive in the world: wisdom, inner calm, patience, and the martial arts. He is their father, but he is also their Sensei, training them in the way of ninjutsu. He cannot watch over them forever, but his stern methods teach the brothers how to rely on themselves and each other.

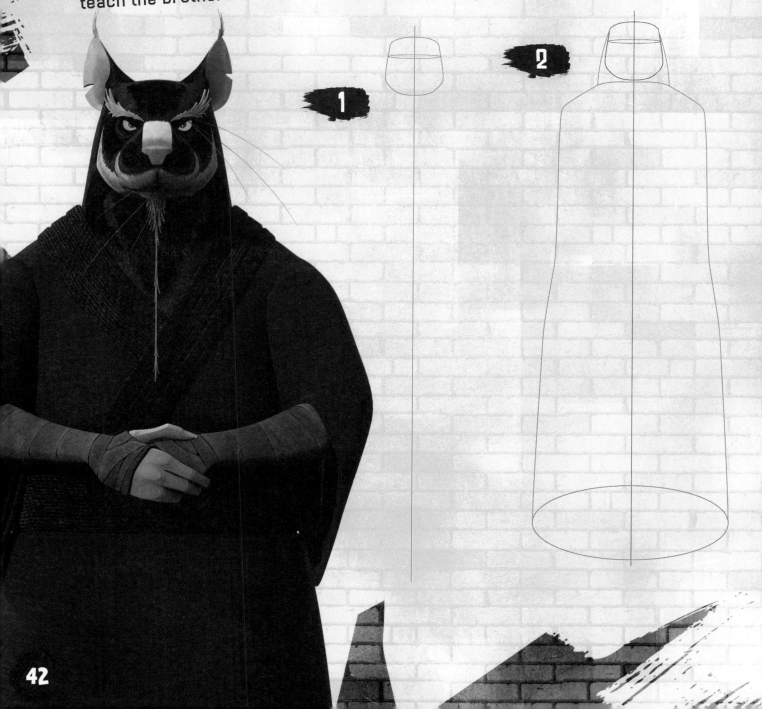

1

2

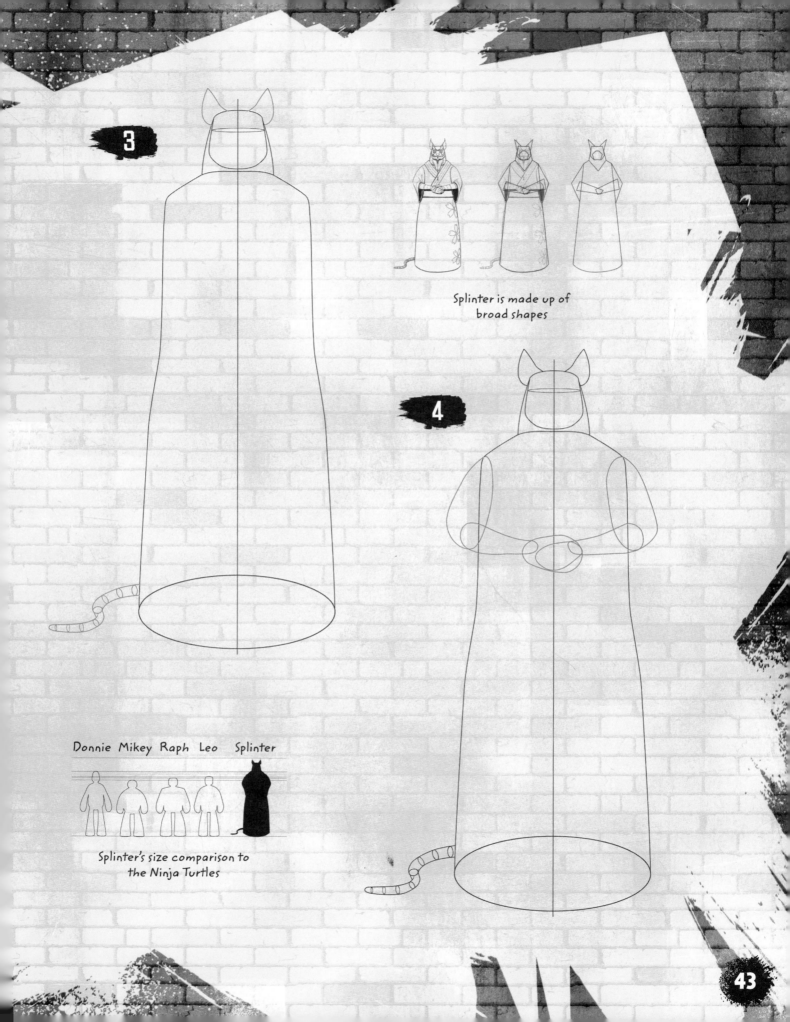

3

Splinter is made up of broad shapes

4

Donnie Mikey Raph Leo Splinter

Splinter's size comparison to the Ninja Turtles

5

Ear details vary in size and position

6

Keep the overall shape of the hair as you draw the details

7

Splinter has 3 flower patterns on his left side

Use squares as building blocks for the hands

SHREDDER

Shredder is one of the most feared kingpins in Japan. A criminal overlord who wears a mask and a suit of armor covered in blades, he is a grandmaster of ninjutsu and the leader of an army of loyal underlings.

1

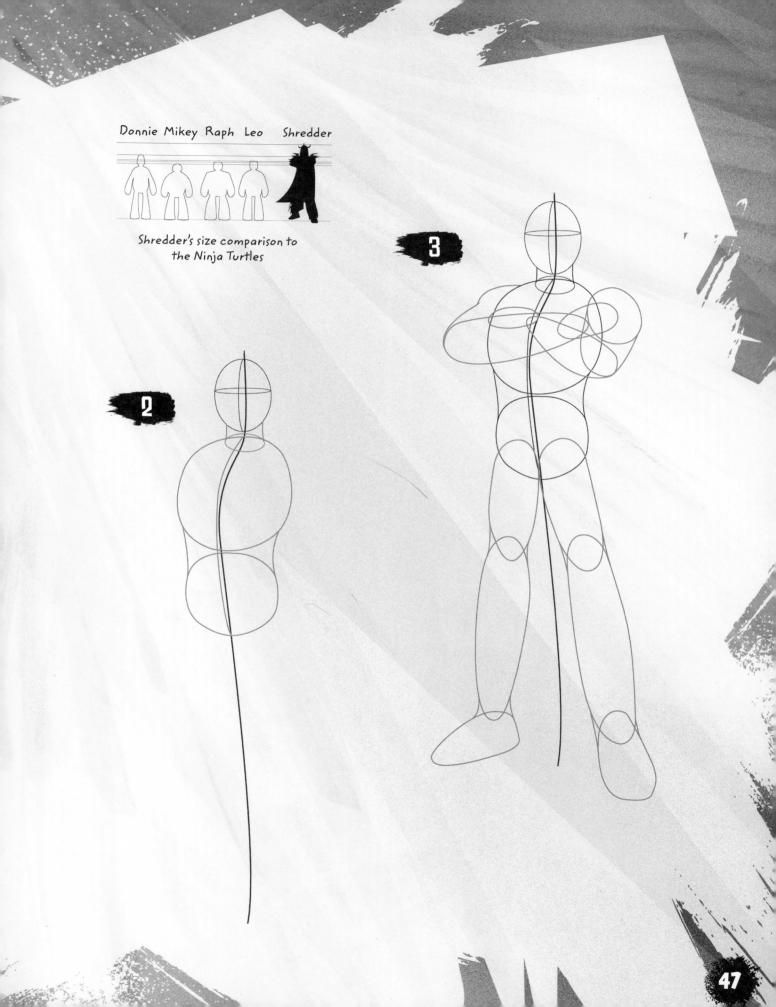

Donnie Mikey Raph Leo   Shredder

Shredder's size comparison to
the Ninja Turtles

2

3

4

Keep in mind
anatomy
underneath
the armor

Shredder's armor is oversized

side view   front view

5

6

Right side of face is scarred

Draw anatomy underneath armor

51

KRAANG

These brain-like aliens from an alternate dimension have one simple mission: to transform Earth into a more suitable environment for their species.

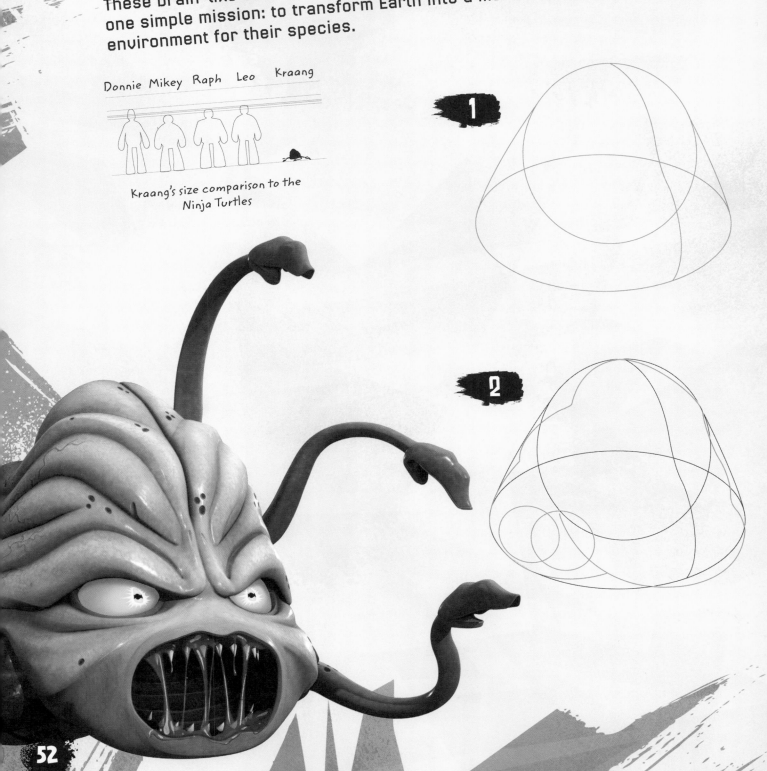

Donnie Mikey Raph Leo Kraang

Kraang's size comparison to the Ninja Turtles

1

2

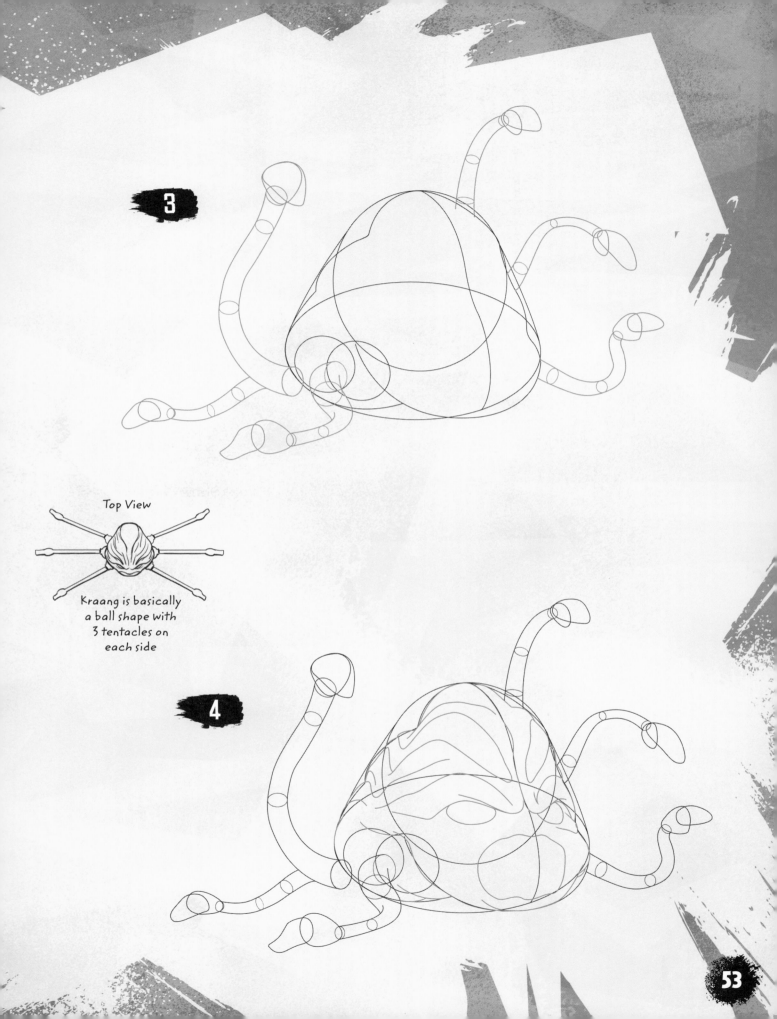

3

Top View

Kraang is basically
a ball shape with
3 tentacles on
each side

4

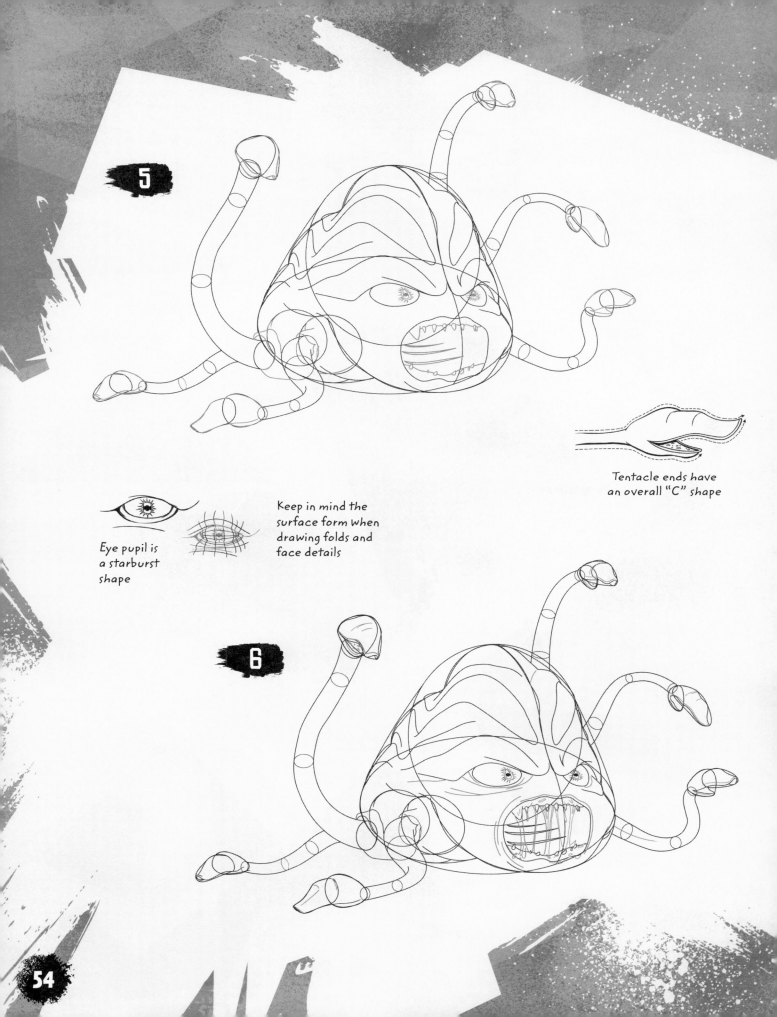

5

Tentacle ends have
an overall "C" shape

Eye pupil is
a starburst
shape

Keep in mind the
surface form when
drawing folds and
face details

6

7

Tentacle base
is basic spheres
and cylinders

APRIL O'NEIL

April is a 16-year-old human who befriends the Turtles after the Kraang capture her father. She is confident that the abilities and uniqueness that her father fostered in her will also serve to rescue him.

1

2

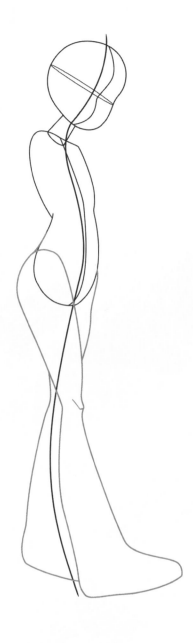

3

Body is shaped like a flour sack

4

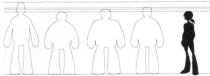

Donnie Mikey Raph Leo April

April's size comparison to the
Ninja Turtles

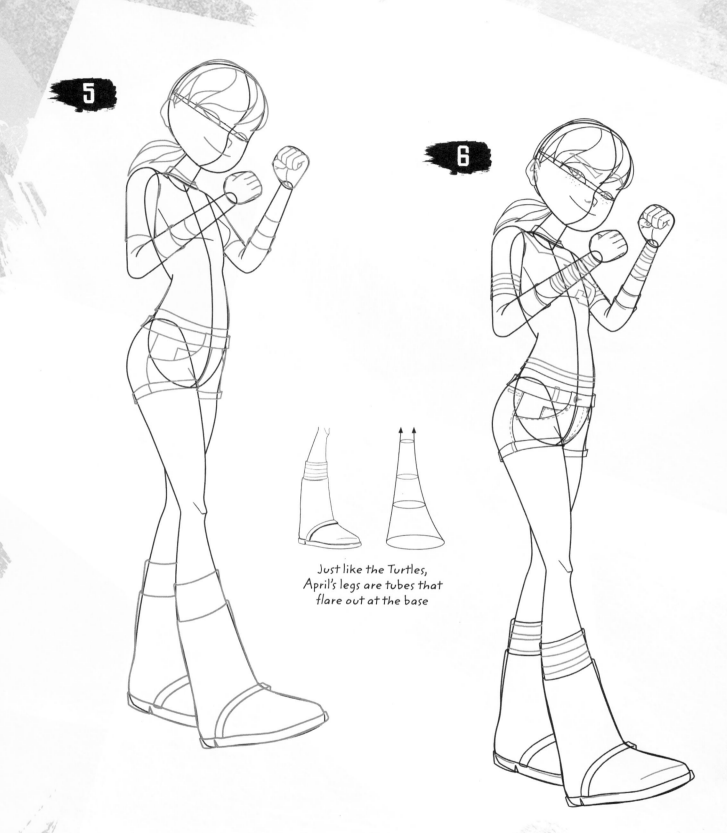

Just like the Turtles,
April's legs are tubes that
flare out at the base

She has freckles on her face

7

FOOT CLAN

As a younger man, Shredder took control of this ninja clan, turning them into an almost invincible horde of thieves. The Shredder maintains his ironclad control of Japan's underworld with his trained army of ninjas, the Foot Clan.

Donnie Mikey Raph Leo Foot Soldier

Foot Soldier's size comparison to the Ninja Turtles

2

1

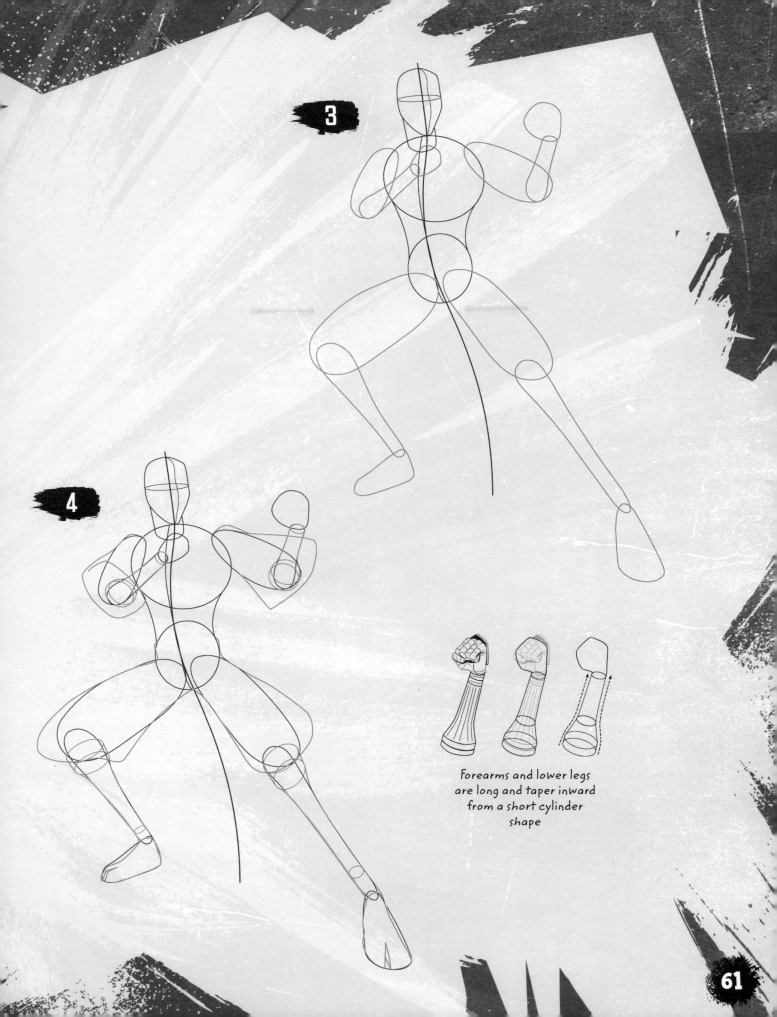

3

4

Forearms and lower legs
are long and taper inward
from a short cylinder
shape

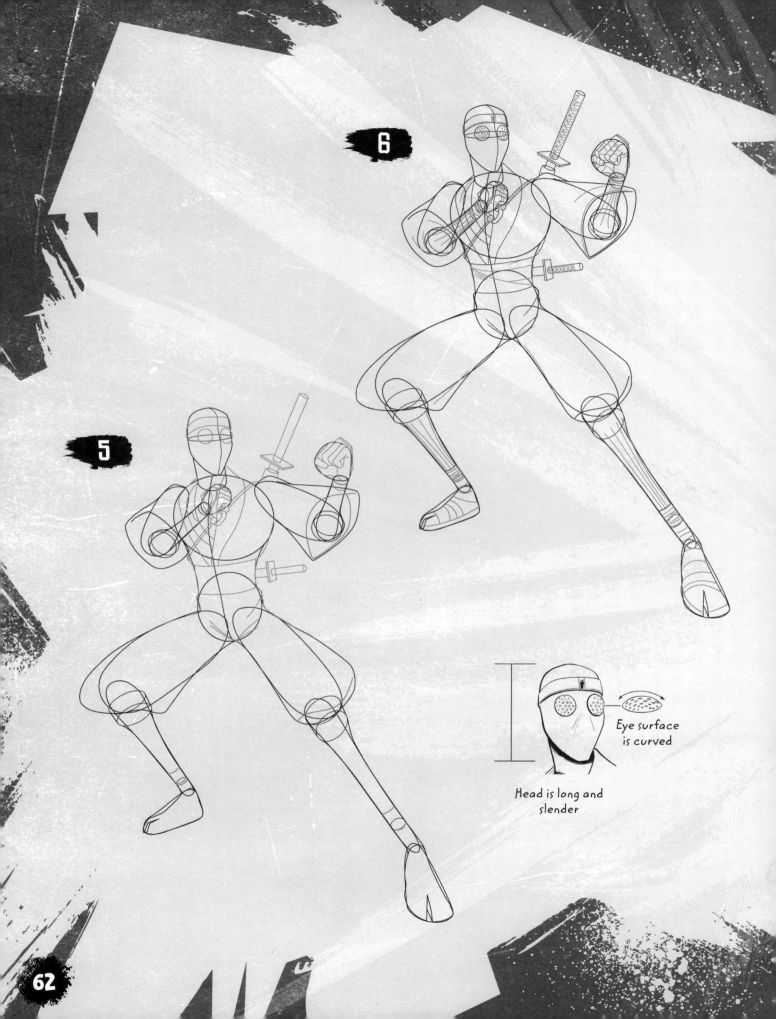

6

5

Eye surface
is curved

Head is long and
slender

7

Use lines of the bandages to give roundness to the form

THE END

Now that you've learned how to draw your favorite characters from the Teenage Mutant Ninja Turtles, try creating scenes from the show or original scenes of your very own. All you need is a pencil, paper, and your imagination!